Why Rec

Blake
EDUCATION
Better ways to learn

Why Recycle?

Go Facts
Why Recycle?
ISBN: 978-1-86509-306-2

Copyright © 2004 Blake Publishing
Reprinted 2009, 2012

Blake Education Pty Ltd
ABN 50 074 266 023
108 Main Road
Clayton South VIC 3169

Ph (03) 9558 4433
Fax (03) 9558 5433

Email: info@blake.com.au
Website: www.blake.com.au

Written by Maureen O'Keefe and Katy Pike
Publisher: Katy Pike
Editors: Maureen O'Keefe and Garda Turner
Design and layout by The Modern Art Production Group
Photos by John Foxx, Photodisc, Brand X, Corbis, Image 100, Comstock, Digital Vision, Art Today, Goodshoot, Image State and Inmagine
Printed by Digital Creative Services

Contents

4  Recycling

8  Paper

10  Glass

12 Cans

14  The Future

Recycling

Why should we recycle?

We use lots of paper, bottles and cans. After they have been used, they can be thrown away or used again.

When we recycle, we use things again. This is good for the **environment**.

People make huge piles of garbage.

Garbage is taken by truck to the **dump**. This land cannot be used for other things, such as parks, farms and houses.

If we recycle, we don't make as much garbage.

garbage truck

city dump

7

Paper

Paper is made from trees.

When we recycle paper, we use fewer trees. Old paper and newspapers can be **shredded** and made into new cardboard.

used paper

plantation forest

Glass

Glass is made from sand and other minerals.

People dig sand out of the ground or sandhills. This can damage the environment. When we recycle glass jars and bottles, we don't use as much sand.

Glass
• Separate by color / Remove Lids.
• Keep Breakage to minimum.
• Container Glass only.
  (No Window Glass, Please.)

Brown Glass

Green Glass

Clear Glass

recycling bins

sandhills

glass recycling

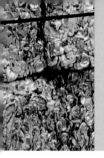

Cans

Cans are made from metal.

People dig **minerals** out of the ground. A lot of heat energy is needed to turn minerals into metal. When we recycle cans, we don't use as much energy.

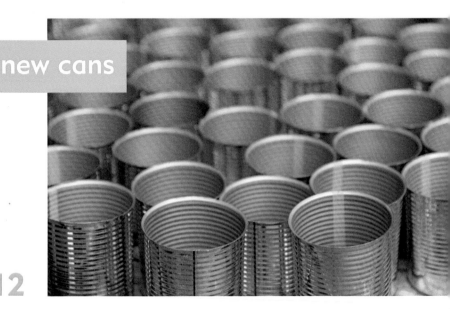

new cans

mineral mine

Cans are crushed, melted and then made into new cans.

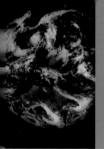

The Future

Reduce, reuse, recycle.

We need to reduce the amount of garbage we make. Recycling helps do this. It also means more trees, minerals and energy for the future.

PLEASE RECYCLE

Glossary

dump a place for rubbish

environment the world around us

minerals things found in rocks and soil

shredded torn into tiny bits

 # Index

cans 4, 12

dump 6

energy 12, 14

environment 5, 10

garbage 6, 14

glass 10

paper 4, 8